Jan Zähler

Lakeside High School - A foreigner's experience with Lakeside High School as example of American High School

GRIN Publishing

Bibliographic information published by the German National Library:

The German National Library lists this publication in the National Bibliography; detailed bibliographic data are available on the Internet at http://dnb.dnb.de .

Imprint:

Copyright © 2012 GRIN Verlag, Open Publishing GmbH
Print and binding: Books on Demand GmbH, Norderstedt Germany
ISBN: 978-3-656-18025-8

This book at GRIN:

http://www.grin.com/en/e-book/192877/lakeside-high-school-a-foreigner-s-experience-with-lakeside-high-school

GRIN - Your knowledge has value

Since its foundation in 1998, GRIN has specialized in publishing academic texts by students, college teachers and other academics as e-book and printed book. The website www.grin.com is an ideal platform for presenting term papers, final papers, scientific essays, dissertations and specialist books.

Visit us on the internet:

http://www.grin.com/

http://www.facebook.com/grincom

http://www.twitter.com/grin_com

Lakeside High School

A foreigner's experience with Lakeside High School as example of American high school

24.02.2012
Antoniuskolleg – English GK
Jan Zähler

Index

1.   Introduction..3

    1.1   U.S. educational system introduction...3

    1.2   U.S. educational system in general...4

    1.3   High School...4

        1.3.1   Graduation in Ohio 5

        1.3.2   Classes 6

2.   Lakeside High School..7

3.   Is Lakeside High School or Antoniuskolleg better? 8

4. Bibliography 12

1. Introduction

I decided to do my Facharbeit about this topic because it really concerns me. The last school year I attended at Lakeside as an exchange student. This experience was amazing and I want to share some of the things I learned. To do so, I will write many things with these experiences I had.

This Facharbeit will be outlining high schools in the United States. To make it more easily understandable, it will also examine the U.S. education system in general. Afterwards the focus will be on high schools, due to the fact that each state differs from each other, Ohio as an example. Lakeside High School will be presented as a sampling of an American high school. This contributes to having taken Ohio as an example state, considering how Lakeside High is located in Ohio and someone needs to know how Ohio high schools are set up in order to understand Lakeside. Finally, a comparison between Lakeside High School and the Antoniuskolleg summarizes this Facharbeit.

1.1   U.S. educational system introduction

"For someone from another country, the U.S. educational system understandably appears large and varied, even chaotic."[1]

This issue happens due to the fact that it is the responsibility of each state to take care of their educational system. Therefore there are differences from state to state: "the responsibility for K–12 education rests with the states under the Constitution"[2] (K grade the kindergarten grade). The Tenth Amendment ensures this by stating that "The powers not delegated to the United States by the Con-

---

[1] U.S. Government, Structure of U.S. Education U.S. educational system understandably appears large and varied, even chaotic, (11.02.12), Online im Internet: http://www.america.gov/st/educ-english/2008/September/20080911223538eaifas0.320335.html, p.1.
[2] U.S. Department of Education, 10 Facts About K-12 Education Funding, (14.02.12), Online im Internet: http://www2.ed.gov/about/overview/fed/10facts/10facts.pdf, p.1.

stitution, nor prohibited by it to the States, are reserved to the States respectively, or to the people."[3]

Furthermore, there are different ways to go through the educational system of the U.S. You can go to high school, secondary school or junior/senior high school. This text will focus on high schools[4], but also address the educational system in general for better understanding.

1.2   U.S. educational system in general

The U.S educational system has a K grade and twelve further grades. Before children in the U.S. go into kindergarten, they can go to a nursery school between three and four years of age. Kindergarten follows nursery school with the K grade at age five. In their sixth year children go to an elementary school for six to eight years, depending on which schools are available in their area. If there is a junior high school, they will leave elementary school in sixth grade and go there. After passing junior high school, children will go to a senior high school, which continues until the twelfth grade. If there is only a high school, children will go to the elementary school until eighth grade and then go to the high school for the remaining four.[5,6]

1.3   High School

The typical American high school takes four years, which are grades nine through twelve. After the twelfth grade students will receive a diploma and can either get a job or go to college.

---

[3] U.S. Government, Tenth Amendment Reserved Powers, (11.02.12), Online im Internet: http://www.gpoaccess.gov/constitution/html/amdt10.html, p.1.
[4] s. Dichanz, Horst, Schulen in den USA Einheit und Vielfalt in einem flexiblen Schulsystem, München 1991, p. 33.
[5] s. Dichanz 1991, p. 32 f.
[6] s. Fiedler, Eckhard; Jansen, Reimer; Norman-Risch, Mil, America in Close-up, 6. Auflage, 1996, p. 188 f.

Even though all students go to the same school, they may have completely different schedules and may receive different diplomas. The graduation depends on which classes somebody took, since each student picks there classes every year in high school.

School starts in the morning and, depending on the times in between periods and the length of each period, it has six to eight periods.

1.3.1 Graduation in Ohio

"The minimum number of credits required for graduation is 23. Of these, 4 shall be in English, 3 in social studies, 3 in science, 3 in mathematics, and 1.5 in health/physical education."[7] This leaves eight and a half credits left for electives. Credits are gained for taking certain classes. Each class usually gives a student a single credit if they take one school year. Those classes that are only taken for one semester, half the year, will give the student half of a credit.[8]

Therefore a student needs to have an English class in all four years of high school. He would also have to have three social studies classes, three science classes and three mathematic classes. However, he can set them up whichever way he likes. A student may take two different social study classes in one year and more in the following year. After that, he does not have to have any more social study classes. On top of these must-have classes, the student needs eight and a half additional credit points to graduate. These can be achieved with electives, classes that a student make take to fulfill the minimum, but otherwise would not have to take, e.g. Concert Choir, Astronomy, Economics and Financial Literacy.[9] In addition to this credit system, the student would need to take a graduation test, which is called Ohio Graduation Test (OGT for short) in Ohio. The OGT consists of five tests, testing Reading and Writing for English, Science, Social Studies and Mathematic skills.[10]This test differs from state to state, which means that if a student takes the OGT and moves to Indiana, he needs to

[7] Lakeside High School, Lakeside High School Scheduling Handbook 2010-2011, Ashtabula 2010, p. 2.
[8] s. Lakeside High School 2010, p. 10 ff.
[9] s. Lakeside High School 2010, p. 14 f.
[10] s. Delisle, Deborah, Ohio Graduation Test Results, in: The Ohio Department of Education, 2010, p. 1 ff.

take the Indiana Graduation Test to graduate there. Once graduated, it does not matter in which state he graduated.

Now a student achieved the basic diploma, but if he wants and is able to get a better certificate, he can graduate with honors. In order to get this better diploma, the student has to fulfill more requirements and also needs to take further tests. There is a diploma with honors and also a Career-Technical diploma with honors. The honor diploma is awarded to general high school students that want to go to college. Those students who wish to acquire a more procedural education can go to a vocational school equal to high school. Vocational schools require some years of high school. It also is advantageous if one is looking to go into a more procedural job. If somebody goes to the vocational school, they can achieve the Career-Technical diploma.

The honor diplomas in general require an additional credit in mathematics, science (also require physics and chemistry at some point), and social studies. A student needs a grade point average (overall letter grades divided by number of courses taken) of at least 3.5, with 4.0 being the best. Likewise, twenty-seven on the ACT or a 1210 on the SAT is required. These tests, the ACT and the SAT, are both additional graduation tests that show how good the student really is. Both diplomas have these requirements in common, but they also differ a little bit from each other. The diploma with honors needs three credits in foreign language classes (if a student has two or more foreign languages he needs at least two credits in each language at least) and a single credit in fine arts. The Career-Technical diploma requires four credits in classes that are apprenticeship oriented. Additionally, this diploma needs another assessment. If a student is able to fulfill seven of these eight requirements, he can achieve either the Career-Technical diploma with honors or the diploma with honors.[11]

1.3.2 Classes

Due to these different opportunities, every student has a different schedule. Some decide to take a class in the next year and some want to take it already. Every high school offers different classes. There are basic classes that every

---

[11] s. Lakeside High School 2010, p.8 f.

high school offers, but varies depending on the money the school has and what their focus is, such as the arts, languages, or science. This means, depending on which school someone goes to, he would have different electives to choose from and this person would get a different education then somebody who lives in a different county.

2.   Lakeside High School

Lakeside High School is part of the Ashtabula Area City Schools. It is located in Ashtabula, Ohio. Furthermore, it has 1154 students and grades nine, ten, eleven and twelve. [12] This already brings it to a special situation. Lakeside is a high school because of its four years. However, there is a junior high school for grades seven and eight. Since a typical junior high school would go from seventh to ninth grade and a senior high school would then go from tenth to twelfth grade[13], it combines two different systems.

School starts at 7:30AM and ends at 1:55PM. There are seven periods over the day and each lasts forty-five minutes. The exception is the lunch period that lasts an hour and a half. Each student will have lunch, but they are split up between X, Y and Z lunch. The students are divided depending on which class they take. Those who have X lunch will go to lunch for thirty minutes and then have their period for an hour. Y lunch students have thirty minutes period, thirty minutes lunch, and another thirty minutes period. Therefore, Z lunch students have an hour period and thirty minutes lunch. All students have to stay in school from the beginning to the end. The only time that somebody leaves is with a teacher or if somebody is picked up by their parent(s) and/or legal guardian(s). Between each period students have four minutes to reach their next class room. If they do not get there within these four minutes, students will be sent to the Student Management Room (SMR). There they have to sit and work on papers the teacher gave them. Furthermore, teachers will send students that disturb the class to SMR. After the period has started, only students with a teacher's

[12] s. Lakeside High School, Lakeside High School Ashtabula, OH 44004 2011-2012 School Profile, in: Lakeside High School, 2011
[13] Ganso, Jan, The American and German educational System: A comparison, München 2002, p.8 f.

pass are allowed to walk in the hall. These passes will be given to the students if the teacher thinks that the reason why the student needs to go somewhere is important enough.

Every student has a personal locker where they can leave their belongings if they do not want to carry it around all day. However, if they leave something there and they need it during the day, they need to find the time to pick it up in between periods.

Class size at Lakeside varies. Depending on which class somebody took, they might have five to thirty other students in there. If they take band, there will be over a hundred students. It really depends on each class.

3.   Is Lakeside High School or Antoniuskolleg better?

There are many differences between both schools. Of course, they both have their ups and downs. However, it is difficult to just say yes to one and no to the other.

The Antoniuskolleg is a much older school. Since Lakeside High was opened 2004 after it was just built, the Antoniuskolleg (AK) cannot compete with Lakeside High. Naturally, the equipment of the AK is good. Nevertheless, everything in Lakeside is new. Likewise, the teachers have their own rooms and every room in Lakeside has computers, an overhead projector and the book sets for the class so students do not have to bring their books to their periods. However, the AK started to upgrade and, even though it will take them a while, they already got some equipment Lakeside does not have, e.g. Smart Boards.

Still, Lakeside's students have their individual lockers where they can put things they do not need for that period. This makes their backpacks much lighter. Students at the AK have to have all their belongings they need for the day with them. This makes their backpacks quite heavy.

Nevertheless, at the AK students can go outside to breathe some fresh air and walk in between a period, which helps them to get focused for the next period. Also, they have longer breaks and fewer periods, helping them to learn more within a week. A student that has to make haste to every period and does not get breaks still has his mind set on the last period. They spend the first fifteen minutes focusing on the new period and it only leaves them thirty minutes of quality working time.

The AK is a Gymnasium, which creates the thinking that students there are nerds and better than the students that go to Realschulen or Hauptschulen. It is needless to say that teachers tell them that this thinking is wrong and everybody has equal opportunities, just different areas. However, it still happens. If you look at Lakeside High where everybody is at the same school, but separated via different schedule, you will still have the conceited thinking. Nonetheless, at Lakeside that thinking is much smaller. It is easier to be friends with someone regardless the grades.

On top of that, Lakeside offers many afterschool activities. The AK offers fewer activities.

In general, it can be said that there is much stronger school spirit at Lakeside than at the AK. Lakeside has its own mascot – a dragon. They have the Lakeside Alma Matter and the Fight Song. These are played just for Lakeside. Furthermore, if there is a football game, a play or a musical, many students try to come to see and support their friends.

Nevertheless, the AK has verbal grades, which really help those who struggle with tests. It motivates students to be working in class, asking good questions, knowing the answers to teacher's questions, being quiet and listening. Lakeside High School leaves this up to the teacher's discretion. Only a few teachers grade in class work.

There is tons of testing in Lakeside High. Having few bigger tests to study for, like the AK has, seems more sensible. Students at Lakeside are seemingly over tested. If there are many short tests following each other on a weekly basis, students study quickly and they know afterwards it does not matter until the end of the year either way. However, if there are only four big tests each year per class, students need to focus on learning so that they remember everything for the tests and are able to be well at them.

Lakeside, on the other hand, has a nice media center with books that will help students with projects and also books just for their spare time to read for fun. Likewise, the AK also has a media center, but there are more books for study purpose only and there are going to be more fantasy novels. This seems better, but Lakeside makes their students read more books than the AK does. Though, the AK works better with the books after they are read. Every student reads a different book in English class at Lakeside while in the AK the whole class reads the same book. This makes it easier to work with the book afterwards.

Students at the AK cannot choose any classes until their tenth or, concerning only a few, eleventh grade. Naturally, it is great that students have the freedom to set up their personal schedule. Howbeit, students might choose something that will influence their graduation in a negative way. Therefore, it is better to give students only parts of that freedom at a later age. This also contributes to the potential that everybody has a similar education.

The teachers at the AK try to keep the student-teacher relationship as neutral and distant as possible. This is supposed to help them make better, fairer grades. At Lakeside the student-teacher relationship is more on a friend base. This has its pros and cons. Some teachers lose their respect in front of the class and cannot enforce their authority anymore. Others are a bigger help for the students and can support them better. In general, there are teachers with no authority in both schools. However, the friendship-based teachers are missing in the AK. Naturally, there are nice teachers in the AK. Having a teacher who actually is there for you, not only to teach somebody in class, but also to be there for you in other complicated situations is helpful.

In the AK, a student has one set class. This means he is with the same people from fifth to tenth grade in nearly every class, which in turn creates a humongous community spirit. Everyone knows each other pretty well after being together for five years. These friendships will last for a life time.

Many teachers at Lakeside hand out a lot of papers over the year. The students do not write as much. Writing is an important part of learning and helps students. It is better to write everything down compared to always getting handouts and later losing them.

At last, Lakeside only has one break. However, this actually seems to be good for students to be more social. They cannot leave the building and need to stay inside. Therefore students have to talk to somebody at lunch and have to be social. This would be good for any student. Besides, if students only have thirty minutes to talk and spend with friends, they spend them way more intensively than more, albeit shorter, breaks.

All in all, both schools are great. However, I prefer the Antoniuskolleg. Naturally, it is great to not only go to school, but also see friends and have a great time. Nevertheless, the goal of a school is to give any student the best education possible in order to reach their future goals. In my opinion, students at the AK will learn more than students at Lakeside.

4. Bibliography

1.) Delisle, Deborah, Ohio Graduation Test Results, in: The Ohio Department of Education, 2010, o.O.
2.) Dichanz, Horst, Schulen in den USA Einheit und Vielfalt in einem flexiblen Schulsystem, München 1991 (quoted as: Dichanz 1991) o.A.
3.) Fiedler, Eckhard; Jansen, Reimer; Norman-Risch, Mil, America in Close-up, 6. Auflage, 1996, o.O.
4.) Ganso, Jan, The American and German educational System: A comparison, München 2002.
5.) Lakeside High School, Lakeside High School Ashtabula, OH 44004 2011-2012 School Profile, in: Lakeside High School, 2011 o.O.
6.) Lakeside High School, Lakeside High School Scheduling Handbook 2010-2011, Ashtabula 2010 (quoted as: Lakeside High School 2010) o.O.
7.) U.S. Department of Education, 10 Facts About K-12 Education Funding, (22.02.12), Online im Internet: http://www2.ed.gov/about/overview/fed/10facts/10facts.pdf.
8.) U.S. Government, Structure of U.S. Education U.S. educational system understandably appears large and varied, even chaotic, (22.02.12), Online im Internet: http://www.america.gov/st/educ-english/2008/September/20080911223538eaifas0.320335.html.
9.) U.S. Government, Tenth Amendment Reserved Powers, (22.02.12), Online im Internet: http://www.gpoaccess.gov/constitution/html/amdt10.html.